EASY GUIDE TO

BABY SIGN LANGUAGE

Always learning.

Table of Contents

Introduction

When you bring a new baby into the world, it is a magical feeling. Especially if this is your first child, you probably cannot wait to share smiles, tell bedtime stories, play and cuddle with your baby. Spending time with your baby is a special thing, for which nothing else could have prepared you.

In six months or so, you will know your baby so well, but you may worry that you do not always understand exactly what she wants. If she happens to be fussy, it may be frustrating for you not to be able to tell what is bothering her.

She won't speak for months yet, but you don't have to wait that long to communicate with her. Baby sign language gives you a means of communication that you both can use months before she will be speaking aloud. It is a rewarding experience to speak to each other when she is still so young. You'll learn so much about her so much sooner than you would otherwise. You'll enjoy the time spent bonding, and you'll feel even closer to your baby.

"Easy Guide to Baby Sign Language" has been written so that you are able to understand and bond with your child as quickly as possible. It has also been designed with the assumption that your free time is very precious. If you only want to learn signs, you can either jump straight to Chapter 4, or use the "Quick Find" indexes at the end of the book. One index is a "Quick Find by Category" and the other is a "Quick Find Alphabetically".

If possible, I would recommend reading the first three chapters first. They provide context to help you understand where baby sign language has come from, where it is going, what the benefits are and how you can set the stage for success. Read on and discover the exciting world of baby sign language!

Chapter One - What Is Baby Sign Language?

History of Baby Sign Language

"Sign with Your Baby" is a program developed in the late 1980s and early 1990s by a student named Joseph Garcia. He discovered that children with a deaf parent would begin to communicate with sign language long before children of hearing parents could talk. In fact, they became expert signers at about nine months of age. However, babies of the same age with hearing parents were not communicating at anywhere near the same level.

Driven by intrigue, Joseph befriended deaf people in his community, committed himself to learning sign language, wrote his Master's thesis on his discovery, and used his infant sons to help demonstrate the positive effect of baby signing.

Joseph's observation would change his life, along with many others. If parents who were deaf could communicate so well with hearing babies, was there also a benefit to teaching sign to hearing children with hearing parents?

At roughly the same time, a PhD at UC-Davis named Linda Acredolo noticed her young daughter "blowing" at fish in an aquarium. It baffled her until she put her child down for a nap later that day. She then realized her daughter had a mobile with colorful fish, and Linda had to blow to make the mobile move. Therefore, her child had communicated with a rudimentary type of sign language. Linda wondered if her daughter was using any other gestures to communicate, and if other children naturally communicated by signing or gesturing.

She would collaborate with a colleague, Susan Goodwyn, and they studied other parents with young children. They received a grant from the "National Institute of Child Health and Human Development", and with it compared infants who signed with those who did not. They followed up with progress notes when the children turned ages two, three and eight.

The results were remarkable. Their findings proved that when babies are taught how to sign, their brains would become more developed. In many comparisons, children who signed would out-perform children who did not. See chapter two for more on the benefits of baby sign language.

The Use of Baby Sign Language Today

Today sign language is used with babies who are hearing impaired and those that aren't. It has been recognized to be helpful in use with children who have developmental delays as well.

Baby sign language enables communication at an earlier than normal age and enhances it. Parents who want the best for their children are using sign language, because communication has been directly linked to cognitive, emotional, behavioral and social development. It can also help eliminate practical frustrations and create stronger bonds. Having strong bonds with your baby is priceless.

Throughout the world, many countries have their own sign languages, and some countries have two or more. Sign language is very similar to spoken languages in that respect, and there are often different dialects too. For purposes of this book, we are focused on using American Sign Language or "ASL" which is the major signing language used in the United States.

There is still much research to be done, but the case for signing is a very strong one. Baby sign language is on the rise domestically and globally due to the many benefits both proven and suspected.

Chapter Two – Baby Signing Benefits

Using sign language to communicate with your baby can create immediate and long-term benefits. The more engaged you are and the more you use it, the easier and more natural it will be. As with many things worthwhile, it will require effort, but I encourage you to stick with it. If you do, there are many rewards to reap. Here are some of them:

Communicate Sooner

The growth that took place inside the womb continues at full speed after birth, and your baby is like sponge absorbing information through all senses. As the senses and the mind develop, your baby will become familiar with her surroundings and the way you interact and communicate with her. It is only natural for her to eventually want to join into your conversations. There is a period of time however when her mind is developed, but she simply cannot communicate verbally. This is because her vocal chords are not developed, and she is still learning how to make sounds.

During this transition period, sign language helps to bridge communication gaps. It opens a whole new avenue of communication that will enable you to develop a much better understanding of your child's unique and amazing personality.

Being able to communicate sooner cannot be understated, because it enables a host of other benefits. Reducing frustrations is one of them and is discussed below.

Remember that every baby will develop at her own pace. Typically people report their children signing at around 8-9 months old, but some people report their babies signing sooner and others later. In contrast, some babies will not speak verbally until two years old or more. Did you know that Einstein did not speak until after the age of two?

Reduce Frustrations

Communicating with your baby using sign language can clear the path for an easier relationship. Babies may be irritable when they want something, and you are not able to discern just what that "something" is. If your baby cannot communicate with you, she will become frustrated which will then frustrate you.

When you and your baby use sign language, your child can tell you exactly what she wants, whether she is thirsty, hungry or wants to play. If your baby is in some sort of pain, it will soothe her if you share the experience with her. You will also be able to address the source of pain more quickly and directly.

Research has confirmed that babies who sign have fewer tantrums and periods of fussiness. And, not surprisingly, you'll feel better at the same time, since you know you are meeting her needs.

Create Stronger Bonds

Baby sign language allows you to understand and interact with your baby at a deeper level sooner. This means you have the opportunity to know each other better and form stronger bonds.

Your baby's eyes are likely to light up when they receive confirmation from you that she has been understood. Repeated interactions like this reinforce that you are able to "get" each other. Also, as she gets older, you will already have a history of communication and experiences to build on.

Some programs for early childhood have even begun using baby sign language as an aid to getting their relationship off to a great start.

Your baby will communicate with you in many different ways, and signing will only be one of them. Signing can add an additional and important means of communication that can complement the others and help you become closer to your baby.

Enjoyment

You will be spending quality time together that can be very fun and engaging. Infants love games and learning, and they will soak up more signs as they become accustomed to this way of communicating. You and your child can enjoy playful interaction, and you'll be able to look on with humble pride at the abilities your child will show.

The key is to be creative, flexible and to come up with your own ideas to engage with your baby's unique personality, interests and environment. In the following chapters, you are taught how to perform various signs, and there are also "Activity Ideas". Use these ideas as suggestions to help get you started.

Enhance Your Baby's Mind and Wellbeing

Communication is fundamental to a baby's development in many ways. It forms the basis of relationships, learning, socializing, playing and more. When she understands and is understood, this can contribute in a positive way towards self-awareness. A positive self-perception can have repercussions of confidence, self-esteem, and positive emotional development. Baby sign language is able to improve communication and therefore has the capability of making an impact in all of these areas.

Some studies also show that babies who learn to sign have a larger vocabulary when they finally learn to speak. In turn, this can improve comprehension, memory, reasoning and judgment. When applied to subjects such as reading, this can certainly aid in academic achievement.

One particular study showed that a group of eight-year-old children who had learned sign language as babies had an average IQ that was 12 points higher than children who did not learn signing as babies.

Communicate in Noisy or Quiet Environments

In times when your child is unable to physically speak, or in areas where voices cannot be heard, you can still communicate with your child. For example, there could be music playing at a noisy party or you might be sitting in a quiet section of a train. Signing will give you the means to communicate anyway.

Communicate with People Who Are Deaf

Globally there are approximately 70 million people who use signing as their first language, and an estimated 1.2 million of them are in the United States. To put that into context, this is approximately the population of Dallas, TX, or more than the populations of Seattle and New Orleans combined. With numbers like these, there are many opportunities for exposure to enriching experiences of the deaf culture.

Become Bilingual

Becoming fluent in ASL (in addition to English) means that your child will be bilingual. When children learn second languages (verbal or non-verbal) it also makes it easier for them to learn other languages when they are older.

Chapter Three – Helpful Hints to Get You Started

Signing with your baby can be fun and simple. To avoid common mistakes, familiarize yourself with these top tips:

Set Realistic Expectations

You may begin signing with your child at any age, but most children will not be able to fully communicate using sign language before they are at least eight months old. Some people do report success several months earlier and others much later. If you don't see immediate results, stick with it. Your child's brain is consuming incredible amounts of information, and it should only be a matter of time before they join in.

Keep Your Signs Simple

Begin with signs that pertain to things in your child's life, like objects and activities. You can also select signs that interest your baby like animals or food. Keeping things simple to start with avoids confusion and provides a foundation to grow and build upon.

Use Positive Reinforcement

Your baby will look to you when she signs, as she does with most everything, for affirmation, acceptance, love and guidance. Responding in a positive way can mean the difference between her learning to sign quickly, and her not progressing as well. When you react to an accomplishment with a sense of pride and excitement, it will make her much more likely to repeat the sign.

Watch your baby to see if she is learning the signs you are trying to teach her. Look closely at any gesture resembling a sign since she may not get a sign right the first time she uses it. Even if you are not sure of the sign, react positively. It's better to give her positive reinforcement over what she can do rather than miss the chance to express excitement at her accomplishments.

Positive reinforcement is helpful with babies, because they want your approval. Praising your child for something she does instills a sense of pride in her. Approval from you and pride in her efforts will encourage her to use more signs.

Use Verbal Communication Too

In order to give context to your signs, sign while you are reading, feeding, diapering or performing other activities. Using multiple forms of communication at the same time will reinforce learning and engrain the sign in the brain. It also provides different memory anchors to draw from in the future.

Be Patient

Your baby may not use signs right away, or she may use them incorrectly. In fact, the gestures they make will most likely be only similar to what you are using. You should never expect that your baby would be able to sign words perfectly. Trying to force her to perfect signs will cause both of you frustrations. With encouragement and patience, your child will sign more easily.

Reactions are More Important than Words

Praise is very important for your baby, but the way you respond to her is more important for her feelings of self-accomplishment. Be enthusiastic and acknowledge her when she signs a word correctly. She needs to know this so she can continue doing the right thing. The more rapidly you respond to her requests, the sooner she will learn that signing is effective in getting what she wants.

If you cannot respond immediately to your child's sign, let her know that you did recognize it and that you will respond as soon as you can. Acknowledge the request and assure your baby that you will take care of it as soon as you can.

Soon, your baby will discover that she will get whatever she needs by signing. This is the beginning of her adventures in signing. When she has this knowledge, your child will be eager to learn more signs, in addition to using the ones she already knows.

Use Signs Instead of Indiscriminate Movements

Many people do choose to create their own signs. In principal, there is nothing wrong with that, but why miss the opportunity to teach them a real language?

Words Can Often Be Signed In Different Ways

There are often different ways of signing the same word. "Dog" has at least five ways in ASL for example. The signs used in this book are real ASL signs, and the focus is on simplicity in order to make it as easy as possible to have quick success. Some books have a mixture of American Sign Language, British Sign Language and made up signs. We haven't taken this course, because we believe there is more long-term value from knowing a single sign. If you know how to speak English fluently, it is more valuable than speaking a little bit of English, a little bit of Hindi and so forth.

Chapter Four – Family

You certainly won't mind some help now and then from family and friends who enjoy babysitting, and you'll want to keep them up-to-date on the signs you are working on with your baby. Aunts and uncles, sisters or friends, your little one will enjoy some of the people you enjoy spending time with, yourself. Your baby will begin to recognize the people she sees frequently. Here are some useful signs to help her refer to and interact with them:

MOMMY

Using your index finger, tap the side of your cheek. Smiling when you use this sign is a good idea, because it reinforces that this is a positive word.

DADDY

Tap your index finger against the side of your face level with the eye.

BABY

Put one hand on top of the other while swinging your elbows from side to side.

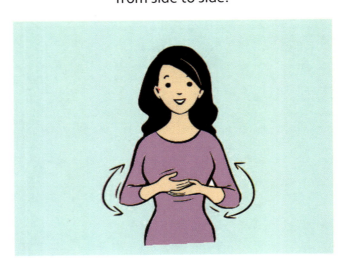

BROTHER

Form an L-shape with the index fingers and thumbs. With one hand at the waist and one touching the forehead above the eye, lower your hand to rest on top of the other.

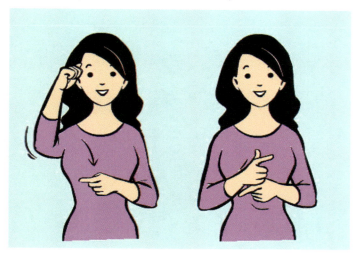

SISTER

Form an L-shape with the index fingers and thumbs. With one hand at the waist and one touching the jaw line, lower your hand to rest on top of the other.

GRANDMOTHER

Extend your fingers and thumb. Starting with your thumb on the side of the chin, move your open hand in a bouncing motion forward.

GRANDFATHER

Extend your fingers and thumb. With your thumb on the side of the forehead, move your open hand in a bouncing motion forward.

AUNT

Rotate your fist in a clockwise circular motion. Keep this below and to the side of the nose.

UNCLE

Make a fist and extent your first two fingers. In position on the side of the head and above the eyes, move your hand in a circle.

I LOVE YOU

With your hand raised and palm facing forward, extend your index finger, pinky and thumb.

KISS

With your dominant hand in the position shown below, tap the side of your face just below and then just above the lips.

HUG

Wrap your arms in towards your chest as if you were hugging someone.

Activity Ideas:

The more you are able to get your friends and family to use sign language with your baby the better. If you are going over for a visit, or if they are coming over to babysit, familiarize them with the signs you have been using. Choose a few simple signs that you think are appropriate, important and that might make life easier. Remember to keep is simple. There is no need to learn everything at once.

For starters, have each family member to learn the sign indicating their relationship with your baby. Your Grandmother will want to know the sign for Grandmother for example. If someone will be babysitting, it may be a good idea to know the signs for milk and other food related items if they will be feeding your baby. Have a look through the chapters in this book to see which signs will be most useful. Family and friends will like knowing that they are contributing to the positive growth of your child, and they can have fun at the same time.

If your family isn't close by, technologies such as Face Time and Skype can allow you to communicate at little or no cost regardless of where you are. I live thousands of miles away from my family and have found these tools to be incredibly effective.

Chapter Five – Food and Drink

Food is something you will always be interacting with which makes it one of the best areas where baby sign language can be used. Your baby will be hungry or thirsty, and as you give them a snack, a drink or a meal, you can converse about what the items are. Here are some useful signs that will help improve your communication:

ALL DONE

Your hands are at the chest level with and palms facing outward. Bring your pinky in towards the body and then flick them outwards as if you are pushing something away.

APPLE

Bring your fist to the cheek. Hook your index finger and twist it back and forth.

BANANA

Create a fist and point your index finger upwards. Then make a motion with your opposite hand like you are peeling a banana.

CEREAL

Extend and curl your index finger several times as you move your arm across the chest. You may also do this with the palm facing down, and motion starting at the mouth.

CHAIR

Extend your index and middle fingers with one hand. With the other hand, curl the index and middle fingers and bring them to rest on the other.

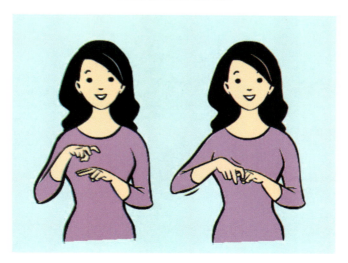

CHEESE

Rub two flat hands together with a twisting motion.

DRINK

Cup your hand like you are holding a drink and bring it towards your mouth.

EAT OR FOOD

Extend and very slightly cup your fingers and thumb. Now tap
the tip of your thumb on your mouth several times.

FORK

Extend your index and middle fingers. Pointing downwards, tap a
couple of times on your other open palm.

HUNGRY

Make a C-shape with your hand at the top of the chest and base of the neck. Then pull it straight down to the base of the stomach.

JUICE

Make a fist and extend your pinkie in the first position below. Then twist the hand around with the pinkie pointing towards your mouth.

MILK

Open and close your fist as if you were milking a cow.

MORE

Cup both hands in the position shown below with your thumb and index fingers touching. Then tap the finger tips together a couple of times.

SPOON

Make a bowl shape with one hand. With the opposite hand, extend the index and middle fingers, and make a scooping motion up and towards the body.

WATER

Form a W-shape using the three middle fingers on your dominant hand. Then tap the index finger against your mouth a few times.

Activity Ideas:

Any time that you give your baby food or drink is a great time to use sign language.

Try taking your baby to the grocery store. She will enjoy riding in the shopping cart, and she will be able to learn about the vast array of foods around her. This is a fantastic place to use sign language.

If you are adventurous, encourage your baby to choose your salad fixings for you. Tell her what each food is as she makes a selection. You may be surprised at what you end up having. There might be some unusual combinations, but they'll probably be quite colorful!

Take your little one up to the salad bar with you at a buffet, and use signing to teach her which foods you like the best. This is helpful to encourage healthy eating when she gets older, too.

Chapter Six - Animals

Children are naturally drawn to animals, especially young ones. They seem to have a built in kinship in some way with small animals, although many very small girls like very large horses too. Animals are an excellent way to help you teach your child signing, because they are naturally interesting and fun. Be sure to use facial gestures and make noises to compliment the signing. Here are some useful and fun animal signs that your baby is sure to enjoy:

CAT

Pinch your finger and thumb together and pull to the side as if you were pulling on whiskers.

DOG

There are five ways to do this, but I recommend tapping the leg twice or snapping with the thumb and middle finger. Your baby won't snap, but you will see the motion.

MOUSE

Make a fist, extend your index finger, and wiggle it back and forth.

RABBIT

Bring your fist to the side of your head. Extend the thumbs, and move your first two fingers up and down.

COW

Extend your pinkie and thumb. Holding your hand above the ear and to the side of the face, rotate your wrist in a twisting motion.

HORSE

Extend the index, middle fingers and thumbs. With your thumbs on the side of the forehead, extend your fingers forward a few times. You can only use one hand too.

PIG

Rest your flat hand under then chin, and cup it several times.

SHEEP

Make a V-shape with your first two fingers, and then rotate them in a circular motion. It is as if you are sheering a sheep.

ALLIGATOR

With one hand on top of the other, your hands should look like the teeth of an alligator opening and closing its jaws.

ELEPHANT

As if you had an elephant trunk. Place the back of your hand against your nose and bring it down and out in a trunk-like motion.

GIRAFFE

Cup your hand around the neck, and extend it upwards.

LION

Fan your fingers out on the top of your forehead, and pull your hand backwards over the top of your head.

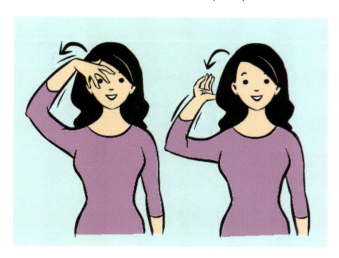

ZEBRA

Wipe your hand across the chest in the shape of the letter Z.

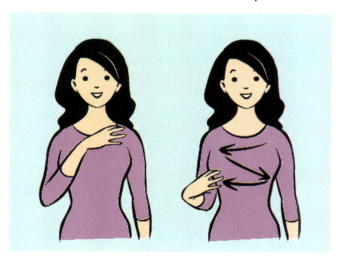

Activity Ideas:

If you have a dog or a cat at home, your child is likely to be comfortable around animals already. Whether you have pets or not, you should still get out there and let your baby experience the wonder of animals. Go to the park, a pet shop or the zoo.

Parks are usually full of people walking dogs, ducks swimming, birds flying and squirrels climbing trees. Sometimes there are horses and other types of animals to see as well. Your baby should love watching and learning more about them.

Pet shops have many different types of domestic animals ranging from fish to guinea pigs, snakes, cats, dogs and more. This can be a great thing to do on a rainy day, because it is indoors.

Zoos are often created with children specifically in mind. There are often areas where children can pet friendly animals, and there are also special events and shows where learning and interaction take place. Close to where I live, a farm hosts an annual nativity play involving donkeys and other animals.

Arm yourself beforehand with the proper signs for any animals your child may recognize.

Chapter Seven – Playtime

When your baby is having fun, there will an extra level of interest in what she is doing and whom she is doing it with. If she sees a ball bounce for the first time, she may be delighted, and laugh uncontrollably as the ball goes all over the place. Now that you have her attention, say "ball" verbally, but also use the sign. She wants to know what it is, so this is the perfect time to engrain the sign into her memory.

The joy associated with playing naturally makes it a great opportunity for your baby to learn. Try to be creative and make things fun.

BALL

Bring your open hands up to your chest facing each other. Now move them in and out towards each other as if you were holding and squeezing a ball.

DOLL

Bend your finger into a C-shape and rub it from the top to bottom of your nose. Then rock your arms back and forth. You may also skip the rocking and rub your nose twice.

HELP

Make a thumbs-up gesture with one hand. Rest it on the palm of the other hand, and lift it up from the waist.

PLAY

Make fists, extend your pinkies and thumbs and wiggle back and forth.

BALLOON

Hold both hands up to your mouth. Then, open the hands out and wrap them around to meet in front of you. It is as if you are running your hands around the outside of a balloon.

FRIEND

Hook your index fingers together. Then do it again by switching which one is on top.

JUMP

Bend your index and middle finger. Now make a motion as if they were your legs jumping and landing on the flat palm of your other hand.

DANCE

Hold one hand palm face up. With your other hand, extend the index and middle finger swing them long ways across the hand.

MUSIC OR SONG

Hold one arm out with a flat hand facing the stomach. Your other hand is flat too, and should wave back and forth almost as if you were strumming the strings of a harp.

RUN

Your index finger from one hand and thumb from the other are touching near the chest. Now move them together in a bouncing motion away from the chest.

SMILE

Your index fingers touch in the middle of the mouth and then move outwards.

SWIM

Move your hands as if you were treading water.

Activity Ideas:

The signs you can do during playtime are endless. If you are playing with a doll, point out the different body parts, and have your baby give it a great big hug. Ask your baby if they would like to hear some music. Then, either play something on your music player or sing them a song. Try to get them to sing along and dance with you. If you have gone swimming, ask them if they enjoyed their swim today. Be sure to use the signs for these words as your go along.

Chapter Eight – Bed Time

One of the biggest challenges of being a parent can be the lack of sleep. Some people are fortunate, and their baby sleeps twelve hours a day while others seem like don't like to sleep at all. Regardless of your situation, establishing a routine for them to wind down and get to sleep is important. Signing can help your baby express when she is ready to sleep and get the routine in place.

BATH

Make fists with both hands and rub them up and down as if you were washing your chest.

BED

Extend your hand and rest it on the side of your face as if it were a pillow. Lean your head slightly to the side as if you mimic the act of lying down. Use one or two hands.

BLANKET

Extend your fingers and tuck your thumbs in. Starting with your hands near the waist, pull them upwards as if you were covering yourself with a blanket.

BOOK

Open and close your hands while in the shape of a book.

GOOD NIGHT

There are two motions. For the first, your non-dominant hand is facing the chest. The other is touching the lips and goes straight down to meet the inside of the other. For the next motion, flip your dominant hand over, and cup it over the top of the other.

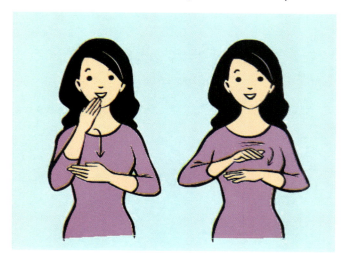

LIE DOWN

The palm of one hand is facing up. With the opposite hand, extend your pointer and middle fingers, and bring them to rest on the palm.

SLEEP

Lower your fingers from the top of the forehead down to the chin. As you move down, make a fist and touch your thumb on the chin.

STORY

Move both hands towards each other. As they nearly meet, make a pinching motion. Pull them apart and repeat the motion.

TEDDY BEAR

Put your hands in the position below and move your hands back and forth in a light clawing motion.

Activity Ideas:

You may want to keep the activity to a minimum during bedtime so that your baby winds down into a restful sleep. Playing too much just before sleep can create too much excitement and a potentially sleepless night.

Reading a book with your baby while they drink some milk and sit in your lap is a great way to make the transition for sleep, bond and help them learn. Let your baby choose which books they would like to read with you. Babies can get distracted easily, and she may want to read several books at the same time. As you move through the books, point at objects, and ask her to tell you what they are.

Ask her if she would like a blanket or a Teddy bear while she is cuddling with you. When you are tucking her in, give her a kiss and tell her goodnight.

Chapter Nine – The Body

As your baby develops, she will gradually become more aware of her body and body parts. Here are some signs you can use to help her understand what they are:

EAR

Hold your ear.

EYES

Point your index finger at your eyes.

HEAD

With your hand on the side of your head and fingers facing the bottom of the chin, move the hand to the top of the head. It is as if you are framing your head.

HURT

Tap your index fingers together a couple of times while rotating your wrists.

KNEE

Hold your index and middle finger down so they look like small legs. Then tap on your knuckle. You may also simply touch your knee, but the first option is helpful if you are sitting at a table of if your legs are not visible.

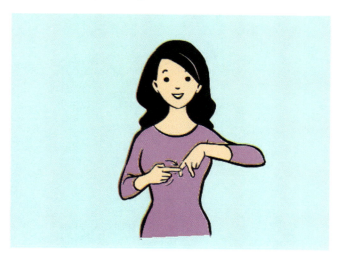

MOUTH

Point and make a circle around the outside of your mouth.

NOSE

Point and touch your nose.

SHOULDER

Touch your shoulder.

TOES

Open your hands, spread your fingers, and bring them to the chest level with palms facing down. Now wiggle your fingers.

Activity Idea:

One of the best ways to teach your baby their body parts is by singing songs with them that require using and touching their body parts. Some examples of songs are "Head Shoulders, Knees and Toes", "If You're Happy and You Know It" and "Hokey Pokey". If you're not familiar with all of these songs, have a look on the Internet. You can pull up a video or two on "YouTube" as well and sing along with a video. Remember that music and songs can be helpful when learning many different signs. In most areas you should also be able to find groups of moms that meet up and sing, sign and play with their babies.

Chapter Ten – Opposites

Learning and memorizing are often easier if an association can be made with something that is already known. This is true whether you are a baby or an adult. Here are some of the most commonly used opposites that you can sign with your baby:

HOT

Cup your hand in a C-shape over the mouth. Then move it away rapidly as if removing something hot away from your mouth. (Please note that this is not the word for spicy.)

COLD

Tuck your elbows in and shiver as if you were cold.

YES

Make a fist and nod it back and forth as if it were you head saying making a yes motion.

NO

Extend your index, middle finger and thumb. Then close them together.

HAPPY

Flatten your hand and rotate it in a circle. Start the circles by moving the hand away from the body and down.

SAD

With both hands at the top of the head, spread and facing towards you, move them down to cover the face. Frown while you perform this sign can bring more clarity.

ON

Your dominant hand is extended and pointing upwards. Fold this hand down to rest on the top of the other horizontal hand.

OFF

Start with the fingers of one hand resting on the top of your other extended hand. Simple lift the hand and flip it over as it moves to the other side of your body.

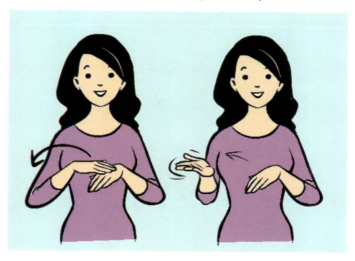

STOP

One hand is extended across the chest with the palm facing up. The other hand should come down in almost a karate chop motion meeting the other hand.

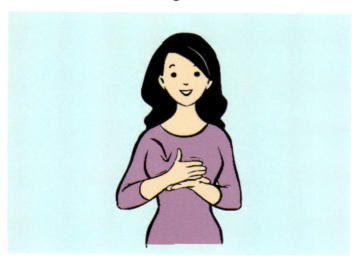

GO

With both hands moving at the same time, point off to one side.

Activity Ideas:

If you find yourself in a situation where you are teaching what something is, and that something has an opposite, try to throw that opposite into the mix. You can sign when you are turning the light switch on and off, when you are saying yes and no, when you are eating food that is hot or cold, and when you are making a happy or sad face or when you stop and go during play.

Chapter Eleven – Manners

Since birth, you have been teaching your child how to understand and share other's feelings. You have been doing this perhaps without knowing it by holding her when she wants a cuddle, feeding her when she is hungry and putting her to bed when she is tired. By responding to her needs, you have been helping her understand relationships, boundaries, and human interaction.

Now is the perfect time for you to teach manners and the signs for manners purposefully, because your baby will love to copy everything you do. If you use the signs for manners and speak them verbally as well, when they do begin to understand their meanings, they will be comfortable using the signs and see positive repercussions.

EXCUSE ME

Bring your fingers and thumb together with your right hand. Then brush the fingertips across the palm of the left hand.

PLEASE

Move your open hand in a small circle around the top and center of your chest.

THANK YOU

Put the tips of your fingers on your lips. With your hand sideways and thumb up, move your hand outwards and down.

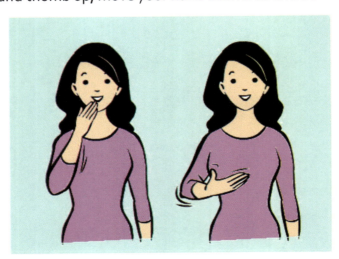

Activity Ideas:

The best way to have a polite child is to be polite yourself. Therefore, use the signs for manners in as many situations and as often as possible. If your baby does something you've requested, promptly say "thank you". Say, "Excuse me" when you need to squeeze by.

Typically first quarrels will arise around toy sharing. This is very normal, but it is still important to encourage them in the right direction. If they would like to borrow a toy, have them use the sign for "please". If they oblige, have them sign "thank you".

Chapter Twelve – Objects

Babies are born with a grasping reflex meaning that if you put something in their hand they will squeeze it. At about three months old, they will begin to selectively reach for things that interest them. Then, as they become more aware of their environment, they will naturally take an interest in the objects you use and interact with the most. It may be your telephone or keys for example. Of course, there will be many other objects that will interest them for a variety of reasons (certainly too many to go into this book), but here are some to get you started:

CAR

Make a cupped C-shape with your hands and bring them together in front of your chest.

BUS

Start with your hands cupped and thumb and fingertips touching as shown. Next move your hands away from each other with the highest coming towards the body.

FLOWER

Pinch your fingers together at the tip of the nostril. Keeping your fingers in the same position, move to your other nostril.

KEY

Hook your index finger and twist it against the palm of the opposite hand.

PHONE

Extend your pinkie and thumb, and pull your thumb up to your ear as if you were speaking on the phone.

Activity Ideas:

The best way for your baby to learn the sign for an object is by seeing it repeated many times while in use, in sight, and clearly the point of focus. You should speak the word out loud when you are signing it as well.

This doesn't mean the object must be physically in front of you. This would be ideal, but seeing it in a book, painting, video, toy or other form can be almost as good as the real thing. If your baby has seen a bus for the first time in a book or video, they are likely to recognize the "real thing" when they see it.

I have never met a child that does not love the song "*The Wheels on the Bus*". Sing this song with them and make the sign for "bus" as you go along. Remember that it is okay to be a bit ridiculous with babies. They don't know the real words to the song. Put a dog on the bus, a Mommy on the bus or an alligator on the bus. They will have a blast, and love using the signs. If there is an appropriate object you want them to learn, why not put it on the bus?

While you certainly don't have to spend money to help your baby learn objects, there are many different toys available that emulate the real thing. There are toy keys and telephones for example. Having these toys can be helpful, because it can prevent her from damaging real items, provide more entertainment value and be less dangerous to use than the real thing. My daughter has keys with buttons that make various car noises. This is fun and engaging for her, and it also helps her associate the keys with the car. If you decide to use such toys, use the sign for that object when asking her if she would like to play with her keys or telephone. When she is done playing with finished, ask her verbally and through sign to please return the item. Use repetition, try to have fun, and she will catch on before you know it.

Chapter Thirteen – Colors

Learning colors can be challenging for babies whether using sign language or not. It is not uncommon to be two or three years plus before things begin to click, but there will always be exceptions to the rule. If your baby isn't able to grasp colors right away, don't worry. She is likely growing and learning about other important things, and it will come with patience and consistency.

Colors can be difficult to learn for several reasons. First, they are often used to describe things such as a blue ball or green apple. This means your baby must know what the object is, what the color is and comprehend that putting the color before the object means it describes that object. This can take some time. It can also be challenging to distinguish between similar colors such as red, pink, and burgundy for example. There are not as many ASL signs for colors as there are in spoken English. You would typically use the sign for red to reflect burgundy for example, and spell the whole word out if required. This would only be possible at a much more advanced stage of course. It is for this reason that sticking with the basic primary colors is a good idea.

Finally, things that make up our world are made up of many different colors with different shades and hues. It may be

obviously to you and me that lips are red, but are they really?
They could be seen as pink, red, even purple or blue to a baby.
When you are teaching colors, try to make sure whatever you are
describing really is that color.

RED

Touch your top lip with your extended index finger. Then pull it
down below the chin.

BLUE

Flatten a hand, tuck in the thumb, and move it hand back and forth as shown below.

YELLOW

Make a fist, extend the thumb and pinkie, and twist the wrist back and forth.

WHITE

Start with an open hand lying flat on the middle of your chest and make a fist.

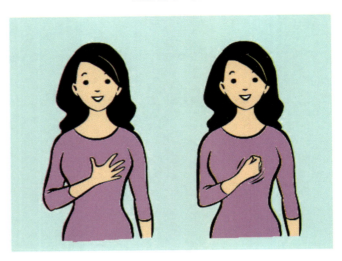

PURPLE

Point your index finger making a small circle in a clockwise motion.

ORANGE

Cup your hand in a claw or C-shape. Then make a fist.

GREEN

Twist the wrist to and fro while almost pinching the thumb and index finger together.

BROWN

With your fingertips pointing up and thumb tucked in, push the hand forwards and backwards slightly while at the side of the cheek.

BLACK

Point with your index finger and wipe it across the forehead.

Activity Ideas:

There are many activities you can do to help your baby learn colors. Using blocks with different colors works well, especially if they fit into your child's hands. When you and your baby play with the blocks, you can teach her the colors as you play. Sit on the floor with her and say and sign the colors of blocks as you and she pick them up. If she is skilled enough to understand, stack blocks that are the same color together. You can even count those blocks, and teach her about counting, too.

Anytime your baby uses crayons, let her know which color she is using. Then ask her to tell you which color she is using too.

You can also buy large bags of plastic colored balls at most toy stores. These are great, because you can hide them and have a scavenger hunt for specific colors. You can also sort them into different color groups, roll them back and forth to each other, and even put them into an inflatable baby pool during the Summer time. Babies love to play with balls, and when you are doing so, use the sign for the appropriate color.

Conclusion

Every parent wants to be able to communicate with her new baby, and using American Sign Language is an excellent way to start. Once your child can communicate her wants and needs to you, life can be much less stressful for you and your baby.

Try to plan times to teach your child signs, and use everyday activities as opportunities. There are so many events that can be used ranging from reading books and eating meals to going to the park or spending time with family members. Try to be consistent and creative, but also be flexible and realistic. Your baby will develop and learn in her own time, but the more involved and consistent you are the sooner she is likely to catch on and reap the rewards.

Quick Find by Category

Family		Food and Drink		Animals		Play Time		Bed Time	
Mommy	25	All done	33	Cat	43	Ball	51	Bath	59
Daddy	26	Apple	34	Dog	44	Doll	52	Bed	60
Baby	26	Banana	34	Mouse	44	Help	52	Blanket	60
Brother	27	Cereal	35	Rabbit	45	Play	53	Book	61
Sister	27	Chair	35	Cow	45	Balloon	53	Good Night	61
Grandmother	28	Cheese	36	Horse	46	Friend	54	Lie Down	62
Grandfather	28	Drink	36	Pig	46	Jump	54	Sleep	62
Aunt	29	Eat/Food	37	Sheep	47	Dance	55	Story	63
Uncle	29	Fork	37	Alligator	47	Music/Song	55	Teddy Bear	63
I love You	30	Hungry	38	Elephant	48	Run	56		
Kiss	30	Juice	38	Giraffe	48	Smile	56		
Hug	31	Milk	39	Lion	49	Swim	57		
		More	39	Zebra	49				
		Spoon	40						
		Water	40						

The Body		Opposites		Manners		Objects		Colors	
Ear	65	Hot	71	Excuse me	77	Car	81	Red	88
Eyes	66	Cold	72	Please	78	Bus	82	Blue	89
Head	66	Yes	72	Thank you	78	Flower	82	Yellow	89
Hurt	67	No	73			Key	83	White	90
Knee	67	Happy	73			Phone	83	Purple	90
Mouth	68	Sad	74					Orange	91
Nose	68	On	74					Green	91
Shoulder	69	Off	75					Brown	92
Toes	69	Stop	75					Black	92
		Go	76						

Quick Find – Alphabetically

A		Cat	43	Fork	37	Juice	38	On	74	Spoon	40
All done	33	Cereal	3	Friend	54	Jump	54	Orange	91	Stop	75
Alligator	47	Chair	35	**G**		**K**		**P**		Story	63
Apple	34	Cheese	36	Giraffe	48	Key	83	Phone	83	Swim	57
Aunt	29	Cold	72	Go	76	Kiss	30	Pig	46	**T**	
B		Cow	45	Good night	61	Knee	67	Play	53	Teddy bear	63
Baby	26	**D**		Grandfather	28	**L**		Please	78	Thank you	78
Ball	51	Daddy	26	Grandmother	28	Lie down	62	Purple	90	Toes	69
Balloon	53	Dance	55	Green	91	Lion	49	**R**		**U**	
Banana	34	Dog	44	**H**		**M**		Rabbit	45	Uncle	29
Bath	59	Doll	52	Happy	73	Milk	39	Red	88	**W**	
Bed	60	Drink	36	Head	66	Mommy	25	Run	56	Water	40
Black	92	**E**		Help	52	More	39	**S**		White	90
Blanket	60	Ear	65	Horse	46	Mouse	44	Sad	74	**Y**	
Blue	89	Eat/Food	37	Hot	71	Mouth	68	Sheep	47	Yellow	89
Book	61	Elephant	48	Hug	31	Music/Song	55	Shoulder	69	Yes	72
Brother	27	Excuse me	77	Hungry	38	**N**		Sister	27	**Z**	
Brown	92	Eyes	66	Hurt	67	No	73	Sleep	62	Zebra	49
Bus	82	**F**		**I**		Nose	68	Smile	56		
C		Flower	82	I love you	30	**O**		Song	55		
Car	81			**J**		Off	75				

99

Resources

http://www.ted.com/talks/patricia_kuhl_the_linguistic_genius_of_babies.html

http://aidenofthetower.hubpages.com/hub/Pros-and-Cons-of-Baby-Sign-Language

http://foodsnobstl.com/2012/01/snobby-mommy-thoughts-on-grocery-shopping-with-a-baby/

http://freshbaby.com/healthy_eating/article.cfm?c=dinner-menus&articleid=219

http://psychcentral.com/lib/teaching-your-baby-sign-language-can-benefit-both-of-you/0002423

http://technorati.com/women/article/why-should-you-add-baby-sign/

http://www.babycenter.com/408_when-can-i-start-teaching-my-baby-sign-language_1368485.bc

http://www.babyzone.com/newborn/new-baby-help-after-having-baby_65670

http://www.deaf-culture-online.com/baby-sign-language.html

http://www.examiner.com/article/baby-sign-language-myths

http://www.examiner.com/article/sign-language-story-time-more-fun-and-learning

http://www.handyexpressions.co.uk/faq.html

http://www.handyexpressions.co.uk/faq.html#usefull

http://www.netplaces.com/baby-sign-language/getting-started/positive-reinforcement.htm

http://www.offspringthing.com/articles/first-trips-out-with-your-newborn/

http://genkienglish.net/teaching/baby-sign-songs/

http://www.hanselman.com/blog/BabySignLanguageUpdateAt2Years.aspx

http://www.mayoclinic.com/health/baby-sign-language/AN02127

http://www.handspeak.com/word/index.php?dict=mo&signID=4676

Can, D. C., Richards, T. L., & Kuhl, P. K. (2013). Brain & Language

Garcia, Joseph. (2010) "Baby Sign Language Research." Sign2Me. Northlight Communications, Inc.

Corballis, M.C. (2002). From hand to mouth: The origins of language. Princeton, NJ: Princeton University Press.

Goodwyn, S., Acredolo, L. & Brown, C.A. (2000). Impact of symbolic gesturing on early language development.

Acredolo, L.P., Goodwyn, S.W., Horobin, K. & Emmons, Y. (1999). The signs and sounds of early language development.

Vygotsky, L.S. (1978). Mind in society. Cambridge, MA: Harvard University Press.

About the Author

J.R. Cagle is a father who wanted to use sign language with his own child. He became frustrated with the poor quality of resources available and dedicated himself to researching this topic. In "Easy Guide to Baby Sign Language", his intent was to make information quickly and easily accessible to busy parents.

J.R. was born in Atlanta, Georgia and lived there for over 30 years. Since 2007, he has lived in and around London, England with his wife and daughter. He is a professional in the Public Relations industry and as well as an acclaimed author and presenter.

Made in the USA
Lexington, KY
16 December 2016